Crush
The Call

Why Some Real Estate Investors Get Deals... And Others Don't

Contents

Introduction

Alright, here's the real deal.

I've been deep in the trenches of real estate investing, and let me tell you, it's been a wild ride.

I've seen some investors absolutely crush it with our leads, while others, using the exact same leads, just can't seem to catch a break.

So, what gives? After some serious digging, I've boiled it down to three main culprits:

1. **Our Leads**: Now, I'll be the first to admit, sometimes a lead might not be golden.

I've had investors hit me up saying we have the "Glengarry" leads (if you haven't watched the movie Glengarry, Glen Ross, put this down and watch it asap), and then I've had other investors say the leads were not working for them, they couldn't get ahold of them, book the appointment or get an ROI.

This dilemma always puts me down the road to continue to optimize our leads to be the best.

2. **Systems and Processes**: Some investors have got their act together with built out systems and top-notch CRMs.

Others?

Well, they're flying by the seat of their pants, and it shows.

3. **Handling Those Leads**: This is where the rubber meets the road.

Some investors just have that magic touch on the initial call.

They get the seller talking, lock in that appointment, and build trust from the get-go.

Others? They can't even get a foot in the door.

So, why am I telling you this?

Because I'm in the game too (I'm an investor) running the same leads and facing the same challenges.

This book? It's my playbook, the steps I take to seal the deal, every single time.

No fluff, no BS, just straight-up insights to help you land more deals.

Because if you're scoring big with our leads, then we're all winning. Let's get to it.

Chapter 1

Who's On The Line?

Alright, here's the deal. I've been in this game for a while, and something's been bugging me.

A lot of investors, even the ones who've been around the block, are dropping the ball when it comes to their sales and lead management game. And the biggest mistake?

Having the wrong people dialing your leads. I'm laying this out because I genuinely want to see investors, like you, get the most out of every lead.

So, let's get to the heart of it: Who's making the calls for you?

I had a bit of a wake-up call when a some seasoned investor sent over recordings of their sales calls for us to review.

And guess what?

I was shocked. They had someone calling from the Philippines with broken English.

Don't get me wrong - a lot of overseas callers are good - but these calls were rough.

The caller talked non-stop for the first 45 seconds of the call.

Hi this is _____ from (company) and I'm calling to find out if you're interested in selling 123 Main St, Pgh Pa 15102 in Allegheny County. Did you have any interest in selling now or anytime in the future...

I'm uncomfortable even listening to the call let alone what the seller is thinking. You figure - they're looking for a cash offer, someone that will BUY their house.

I've found that most sellers are looking for someone local that seems reputable that can actually buy their house. They're not looking for people to rip them off - and when this is your first touch, it can draw flags and make them feel like they're talking with the wrong place.

But...All leads should not be handled the same

Think about where your leads are coming from and how much they're costing you. If you're playing the numbers game with SMS or cold calls, sure, you might not want to spend big bucks on each caller.

But if you're shelling out a good chunk of change for each lead, do yourself a favor: get someone skilled, preferably stateside, to make that first impression count.

It could be the difference between a 'maybe' and a 'heck yes!'.

Chapter 2

The CRM Game-Changer

Every real estate investor, and I mean every single one, needs a CRM. Which one?

Honestly, there are so many options, if you're not using one tho - just get one! (don't get paralysis by analysis here)

I'm currently using Go High Level. REI Simpli, Podio, Salesforce, Follow Up Boss?

They're all solid choices.

The bottom line is, you've got to have one.

If you're in the dark about this, give me a shout.

I'll hook you up and get you rolling.

Now, why is this so crucial?

Picture this: You've got leads pouring in. Out of every 10, maybe one is ready to sell right away.

But what about the other nine? They're interested, but the timing's off.

It could be a week, a month, half a year, or even longer.

That's where your CRM steps in, acting like your personal organizer.

Take John, for instance. You chat with him, and he mentions he's not selling until three months down the line because he's waiting for his daughter to graduate college.

Pop that into your CRM. Note down the reason.

When those three months are up, your CRM nudges you. It's time to ring John.

And thanks to your notes, you can pick up right where you left off.

"Hey John, congrats to your daughter on her graduation!"

It's personal touches like these that make all the difference. Without a CRM, you're relying on memory (if you even remember to call)

And here's the thing. Most sellers are not going to remember talking with you a few months later, so things like this let them know you actually talked in the past.

To wrap it up: A CRM isn't just important; it's essential.

Without one, you're basically leaving cash on the table.

And the best part? CRMs won't burn a hole in your pocket.

So, if you don't have a CRM at the moment, stop reading this, go get one and then come back!

Chapter 3

The Calendly Advantage in Lead Management

Let's dive right in. If you're not using Calendly for managing your leads, you're missing out.

Big time!

Here's how I roll: The moment a lead pops in, I shoot them a text. It goes something like, "Hey there, thanks for reaching out. Click on this link, and you can directly book a time for us to chat and get you an offer."

BTW - you can automate this ^

Think about it. Someone's up at 3:00 AM, probably can't sleep, and they're thinking about how to offload their property fast.

They stumble upon your ad, fill out the form, but then what?

Most likely they're going to go the next site they see and fill out their form too!

But, if right after they hit 'submit', they get a text with a direct link to your calendar?

Boom! They're locked in.

They set up an appointment, feel like they've accomplished what they were looking for, and hit the sack.

This isn't just about convenience; it's strategy. It's about making sure that lead doesn't drift away to a competitor.

It also helps you gauge motivation. What type of person is going to book an appointment with a stranger to come to their house? A motivated one!

Now, for those of you looking for a solid script, here's mine. Feel free to swipe it:

I have this SMS go out immediately. Make sure to link your Calendly at the bottom so they can set up an appointment with you.

Hi (name),

Thanks for the message about selling your house.

Here is a link to our live calendar to set up an appointment to give you an offer.

Pick any day and time that works for you!

(Your Calendly here)

Your Calendly

Notice I ask a lot of the same questions again - I recommend doing the same on your side. Copy it exactly as I have it:

Enter Details

> **Name ***

> **Email ***

> **Phone # ***

> **What is the address of the property you would like to sell? ***

> **City ***

> **Zip Code ***

> **Why do you want to sell your property? ***

> **Does any work need to be done to your property? ***

> **What are the mortgages/liens on the property? ***

> **Is your property already listed with a realtor? * (Yes or No)**

> **How did you find us? Google, Facebook or Mailer? ***

> - **Please confirm that you are aware that someone from (your company) will be coming to your property on [time, date] the appointment is scheduled. * (Yes or No)**

I'm going to hammer this point home: Speed is everything with online leads. The faster you lock them in, the better your chances. So, get on it!

Chapter 4

Crafting a Seamless User Experience

Alright, let's dive into a golden nugget of advice that can make a world of difference: enhancing user experience.

Imagine this: someone lands on your website, fills out a form, and then... what?

They're left wondering, "Now what?" That's where you step in with a smooth transition.

Here's a game-changer:

On your 'Thank You' page, Put on a button linking straight to your calendar.

But don't stop there.

Add a video – a brief one, nothing too lengthy – thanking them and laying out the next steps.

"Thanks for filling out a form. If you look below - you'll see a button to book an appointment. Go ahead and book that and what will happen next is we'll call you to confirm your appointment and then we'll meet at your house to give you a cash offer."

The beauty of this approach? Clarity.

You're not just asking them to book an appointment in the dark.

You're guiding them through the process, step by step. It's like giving someone a roadmap.

They're more likely to embark on a journey if they know the path.

And trust me, people are way more relaxed when they know what's coming up.

So, don't play your cards too close to your chest. Be upfront. Be transparent.

And here's another pro tip: After they've booked that appointment, hit them up with another video. Dive a tad deeper into the details.

"Hey there, thanks for setting up a time. Here's a quick breakdown on what happens next...."

And lay it out for them.   Put whatever your process is but keep the video less than 2 min or so.

The goal? Building trust. You want them to feel like they're in good hands.

The more they know, the more at ease they'll be.

And in this business, a comfortable seller is a game-changer.

So, lay it all out, and watch the magic happen.

Chapter 5

The Art of the Initial Call

Let's get one thing straight: diving straight into price talk on your first call with a seller?

You'd be surprised how many calls I listen to where the investor jumps directly into "how much do you want"

Not the best move.

I'm talking some people are asking this 30 seconds into the conversation.

Here's how I handle it, and trust me, it's a game-changer.

First off, genuinely care.

These are REAL PEOPLE with REAL PROBLEMS.

I'm a helper by nature, so this comes naturally to me, but what I like to think is that I'm like a doctor, trying to find out what your problems are so I can come up with a **win/win solution** to solve them for you.

So, let's break down my script:

*"Hey, it's Bryan. Noticed you filled out our online form. Good time to chat? Awesome.

The purpose of this call is to learn about you, your property and situation and also answer any questions you have about me and how this works.

At the end of the call - if you don't think this is a good fit, you can just tell me that and we'll part as friends....

You won't hurt my feelings.

Are you ok telling me that if you don't think it's a fit?

(and then I wait for them to reply)

But... at the end of this call it does seem like a fit, we'll set up a time to meet up at your house & check it out.

Once we do that - I'll be able to give you a cash offer and hopefully we make a deal.

Sound good?

That's an upfront contract. I'm setting the stage, letting them know what to expect, and ensuring there's no pressure.

I'm also getting commitment that they will give me an answer at the end of the call.

They are either agreeing to meet and we'll move to the next stage, or they're going to tell me no.

This is important. If they're not going to do something - you want them telling you no.

This saves you and your team hours of follow up on a deal that will never happen.

So don't be afraid to tell them it's ok to tell you "it's not a fit"

You're doing yourself and the seller a favor.

Next - I dive into my questions:

"So, why do you want to sell?" And then, I zip it.

A lot of people ask questions, then if there is 5 seconds silence after - they talk again. Don't do that!

Listen more than you talk. You're trying to uncover their real motivation.

And when they start talking - listen hard (because this is where the deal is going to be made)

People sell for all sorts of reasons.

Maybe they're swamped with work and just inherited a fixer-upper they can't handle.

Maybe they're behind on payments.

Maybe they're a hoarder and don't want their neighbors walking through the house if it goes on the market.

Your job? Find out what's driving them.

Then, gauge their urgency with, *"How quickly are you looking to sell?"* This helps you understand if time is a major factor for them.

Next up, the price. I casually ask, *"How much are you looking for?"* Not because I'm fixated on the number, but to get a feel for their expectations.

Now, let's talk property details. Questions like,

How old is the roof?

How old are the windows

How old is the furnace

Do you have circuits or fuses

Any termites?

Any recent updates?

Does the basement get water?

I like to ask these types of questions to get a sense of the property and what work THEY think it needs.

And remember, when someone says "minor repairs," it might mean a whole lot more.

Throughout the conversation, keep your detective hat on.

You're trying to piece together their real motivation to sell.

Is it time? Money? Something else entirely?

Lastly, get into the nitty-gritty.

Ask about mortgages, how much they owe, and if they're the sole owner.

This ensures you're talking to the right person and that they're in a position to sell.

Toward the end of the call - I like to ask another question.

I've made hundreds of thousands of dollars by just asking this next question.

So... What's the best price you'd do for a cash offer. (again, shut up and enjoy the awkward silence)

I'm still not gauging the price. What I want to see is how much did the figure change from the beginning of the call to the end.

For example - if they said they need 110k at the beginning of the call and then they tell me the best price is 108k, I'm not seeing much motivation or wiggle room, but this allows me to probe more.

Maybe their mortgage balance is 108k. Who knows.

But... If they wanted 110k and then they say: Well, if we could do as-is and close fast, I'd prob do 85-90k. Now your baseline is 85k.

You will make more money in the 30 seconds by asking that question than most things in life. You figure - in the example above - that's 25k difference.

Remember, this initial call is all about building trust, understanding their needs, and setting the stage for a potential deal.

So, listen up, ask the right questions, and always, always care.

Chapter 6

Transparency and Integrity in the Deal

Alright, let's get into the meat of the conversation: explaining your role and intentions. This is where clarity and honesty are paramount.

Usually, I lay it out like this:

"I'm a cash buyer. That means I've got the funds ready to buy your property. We can close quickly or take our time, depending on what suits your situation.

But here's the key: I'm the actual buyer. I'm not the middle man that has to find someone else to buy it.

If we agree on a price, we're going to close. No waiting for financing or any other hurdles."

Now, if you're a wholesaler, **it's crucial to be upfront about it**.

Something like, "I'm a wholesaler. I do buy properties, but I also have a network of investors who might be interested.

I'll market your property to them, and regardless of whether I find a buyer or not, we'll close in 30 days." The point is to be crystal clear about your role and intentions. Tailor this to your situation.

Being transparent isn't just ethical; it's smart business.

I've seen situations where wholesalers ask me to pretend to be a contractor when inspecting properties. That's not my style.

It's not just about feeling uncomfortable; it's about doing right by the seller. Selling a home is a significant life event, and they deserve honesty.

And here's a golden rule: If you commit to buying a property, ensure you can close the deal. Think about it.

The seller might be making life-altering decisions based on your word.

They could be hiring movers, signing new leases, or making other arrangements.

If you back out last minute, it's not just a business hiccup; you're impacting someone's life.

In this game, your reputation is everything. Be transparent, be honest, and always, **always follow through on your commitments.**

Chapter 7

The Power of Promptness

Let's wrap this up with a crucial piece of advice: Speed matters. A lot.

Once you've had the initial conversation, the next step is to see the property. And here's where many investors drop the ball. They delay.

They schedule a visit days or even weeks later.

But here's the thing: if a seller is reaching out, they're likely talking to multiple investors.

And if you're not the first one at their door, you might just miss out.

My approach? Strike while the iron is hot.

If a seller is keen, I aim to visit the property the very same day.

Why?

Because if they're motivated to sell, they're looking for solutions now, not next week.

By being the first investor they meet face-to-face, you not only get a head start, but you also show them you're serious and responsive.

Consider this: A motivated seller is likely feeling some level of stress or urgency.

They might have filled out multiple online forms, and other investors might be ringing them up.

If you can be the first to visit, assess, and potentially make an offer, you're in a prime position.

In this business, every minute counts.

A motivated seller is looking for fast solutions.

By being prompt, proactive, and present, you're not just increasing your chances of sealing the deal; you're also alleviating the seller's stress.

And that, my friend, is a win-win.

Conclusion

The Heart of the Deal

To sum it all up, the initial interaction – from that first phone call to the person making the call, and the pace at which things progress – is absolutely pivotal.

It's the foundation upon which successful deals are built.

I can't stress enough how vital it is to give this phase of your business the attention it deserves.

It's not just about making a sale; it's about building trust, understanding needs, and acting swiftly.

If you get this right, you're not just closing more deals; you're maximizing your profits and building a reputation as a reliable, efficient investor.

For those of you looking to generate more leads or seeking insights into refining your sales process, don't hesitate to reach out.

At MotivatedLeads.com, we're here to help, guide, and ensure you're on the path to success.

Remember, in real estate, it's not just about properties; it's about people.

And that first call?

It's where it all begins.

www.ingramcontent.com/pod-product-compliance
Lightning Source LLC
Chambersburg PA
CBHW072230290526
45794CB00007B/2956